BRUCE SPRINGSTEEN

A Little Golden Book® Biography

By Laurel Snyder

Illustrated by Jeffrey Ebbeler

🖼 A GOLDEN BOOK • NEW YORK

Text copyright © 2023 by Laurel Snyder
Cover art and interior illustrations copyright © 2023 by Jeffrey Ebbeler
All rights reserved. Published in the United States by Golden Books, an imprint of
Random House Children's Books, a division of Penguin Random House LLC, 1745 Broadway,
New York, NY 10019. Golden Books, A Golden Book, A Little Golden Book, the G colophon,
and the distinctive gold spine are registered trademarks of Penguin Random House LLC.
rhcbooks.com
Educators and librarians, for a variety of teaching tools, visit us at RHTeachersLibrarians.com
Library of Congress Control Number: 2022942330
ISBN 978-0-593-56980-1 (trade) — ISBN 978-0-593-56981-8 (ebook)
Printed in the United States of America
10 9 8 7 6 5 4 3 2 1

BRUUUUCE!

Bruce Frederick Joseph Springsteen was born on September 23, 1949, in New Jersey. He grew up in a small town called Freehold, not far from the ocean.

Bruce lived with his mom and dad, his two sisters, and sometimes his grandparents, too. Their little house wasn't very fancy—just four rooms. The bathroom sink didn't even have hot water! But there was a gigantic beech tree in the yard that Bruce loved to climb.

Each day, Bruce walked down the street to the St. Rose of Lima Catholic School, where he often got in trouble with the nuns who taught his classes. Bruce was full of energy, and he had a hard time sitting still. He was much happier riding his bike down the cracked sidewalks or playing with his friends.

Bruce loved gutterball. Have *you* ever played gutterball?

When Bruce was seven years old, he heard a man singing on TV. The man's name was Elvis Presley, and the song was called "Hound Dog."

"You ain't nothing but a hound dog," sang Elvis, twisting his hips and curling his lips.

Bruce was amazed! He tried twisting his hips and curling his lips. He begged his mom for a guitar.

Bruce's mom didn't have enough money to buy a guitar, but she rented him one. It cost six dollars a week. Bruce was excited to play, but it sounded all wrong. *TWANG!* Also, it made his fingers hurt.

On the morning he had to return his guitar, Bruce gave a concert for some kids in the neighborhood. He couldn't really play, but that didn't stop him. Bruce danced and jumped and shouted. He didn't sound great, but he sure had fun!

Even though the guitar was gone, Bruce never stopped dreaming of music. He had rock and roll in his soul!

Bruce spent hours at a local luncheonette, singing along with the jukebox. When he had extra money, he bought records at the five-and-dime store. And in bed at night, he fell asleep listening to his transistor radio.

Bruce loved all kinds of music, but his favorite songs were the ones that sounded happy and sad at the same time.

Bruce mowed lawns and painted houses. He saved up his money, and before long bought his very own guitar for eighteen dollars.

This time, Bruce didn't let his sore fingers get in the way. He played and played. It wasn't easy, but he found some books to learn from. The very first rock and roll song he learned to play was "Twist and Shout," by the Beatles.

Now Bruce played his guitar all the time. The more he played, the better he got.

But if he wanted to play in a real band, Bruce would need an electric guitar, and he definitely couldn't afford that. So Bruce sold his pool table for thirty-five dollars, and his mother agreed to give him the rest of the money he needed. Together, they bought the guitar.

Bruce and his band played at a high school
dance. It didn't go well at all. They sounded terrible!
But Bruce kept at it. Over the next few years,
he played in a lot of different bands. He played at
dances, beach parties, and teen clubs. He played
wherever he could.

Then one day, when Bruce was nineteen, his dad decided it was time for a big change. He wanted to move the whole family to California! Bruce didn't want to leave his home and his band. He decided to stay behind in New Jersey.

With the house empty, Bruce's band moved on in, but they had to move right back out again!

The neighbors didn't appreciate living next to a bunch of messy teenagers with noisy guitars. So Bruce and the band packed up their things and drove down the road a ways, to a town called Asbury Park, where there was a sandy beach, a boardwalk, and music every night.

There, Bruce and his friends
played for small crowds of people.
Then bigger crowds of people.
And then even bigger crowds
than THAT!

BRUUUUCE!

When he wasn't performing, Bruce wrote songs about people and places he knew. He wrote about his family and his town, about the hard work people did, and also about the things they dreamed of doing.

Bruce wrote about faraway places he'd never been to, and the highways he hoped would take him there.

As the years passed, Bruce's band sometimes changed names and members.

One night, a saxophone player named Clarence sat in. When he and Bruce played their first notes together, it was like magic! Bruce and Clarence "the Big Man" Clemons would be friends forever.

A few years later, a beautiful redhead named Patti Scialfa joined the band. Bruce liked her a lot.

No matter who came and went, Bruce kept writing his songs and playing his guitar. *That* didn't change.

Now Bruce was a rock star! With his
E Street Band, he recorded loads of hit songs,
like "Hungry Heart" and "Born to Run." He
sold hundreds of millions of records.

Bruce played concerts all over the world.
Sometimes he played for four hours, dancing
and jumping and shouting. The crowds loved
every minute!

Eventually, Bruce moved to California, where he and Patti decided to get married. They started a family, and had three children together—Evan, Jessica, and Sam.

Bruce has won lots of awards, including twenty Grammys, an Oscar, and a special Tony Award for his show *Springsteen on Broadway*. He was voted into the Rock & Roll Hall of Fame. And in 2016, President Barack Obama presented Bruce with the Presidential Medal of Freedom. The two became good friends.

Bruce had everything he could want. He was rich and famous. He had family and friends. The only thing missing was home.

So Bruce decided it was time . . .

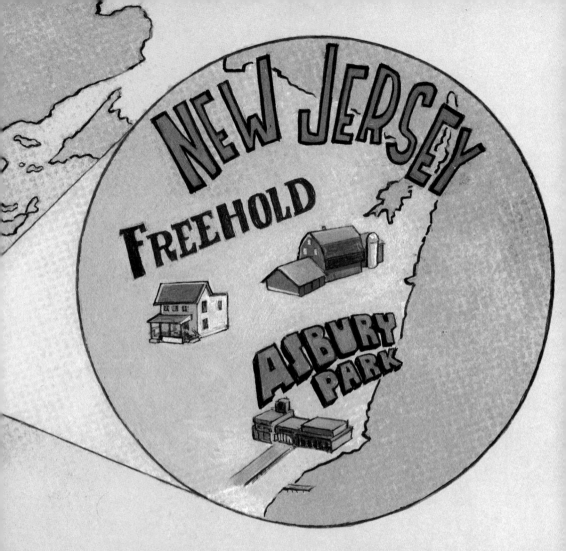

. . . to go back to the place that had inspired his songs and his life—New Jersey!

Bruce and his family moved to a farm just down the road from Freehold, not far from the ocean.

In fact, that's probably where he is right now, this very minute—living, dreaming, and working hard, just like always. He's playing his guitar and writing new songs, just like always, and singing, singing, singing . . . just like always. Bruce still has rock and roll in his soul.

Thank goodness, *some* things never change.